How to Create the Inclusive Classroom

How to Create the Inclusive Classroom

Removing Barriers to Learning

Rita Cheminais

 David Fulton Publishers

David Fulton Publishers Ltd
The Chiswick Centre, 414 Chiswick High Road, London, W4 5TF

www.fultonpublishers.co.uk

First published in Great Britain in 2004 by David Fulton Publishers

10 9 8 7 6 5 4 3 2 1

Note: The right of the author to be identified as the author of this work has been asserted by her in accordance with the Copyright, Designs and Patents Act 1988.

David Fulton Publishers is a division of Granada Learning, part of ITV plc.

Copyright © Rita Cheminais 2004

British Library Cataloguing in Publication Data
A catalogue record for this book is available from the British Library.

ISBN 1 84312 240 5

Designed and typeset by Matrix Creative, Wokingham
Printed and bound in Great Britain

How to Create the Inclusive Classroom
Removing Barriers to Learning

Rita Cheminais

Contents

Chapter 1

National Inclusion Framework

What makes inclusion work?

Removing barriers to achievement

Every child matters

Disability, access and inclusion

Access and inclusion – SEN and Disability Act 2001

National Curriculum inclusion principles

Assessment and inclusion

Assessment, target setting and inclusion

Features of the ideal inclusive school

Features of inclusive schools

SEN in mainstream inclusion checklist

Chapter 2

Inclusive Classroom Practice

Inclusive learners' entitlement

Inclusive classroom climate

Including and empowering the pupils

Empowering the SEN pupil

Pupils' inclusive learning audit

Teachers' inclusive learning audit

Inclusive learning – teacher checklist

Learning retention

Effective inclusive learning approaches

Learning styles

The learning cycle

Accelerated learning approaches

Whole-brain learning

Chapter 2 cont.

Left and right brain activities

Multiple intelligences for all learners

Thinking skills for all pupils

What inclusive classroom practice looks like

Ideas for promoting inclusive practice

Reducing barriers to learning and participation

How accessible is your classroom?

The Government's Strategy for SEN

Classroom strategies for including pupils with ASD

Classroom strategies for including pupils with BESD

Classroom strategies for including pupils with SLCD

Classroom strategies for including pupils with learning difficulties (MLD, Sp.LD)

Chapter 3

Inclusion Roles and Expectations

Headteacher role and expectations

SENCO role and expectations

SENCO role and inclusion

SENCO's evolving inclusion role

SENCO/INCO role

NQTs' roles and expectations

Teachers' roles and expectations

Teaching Assistants' roles and expectations

Effective deployment of TAs

Pupils' roles and expectations

Parents'/carers' roles and expectations

Governing body role and expectations

Outreach/external professionals' roles and expectations

Transition, SEN and inclusion

Chapter 4

Reviewing Inclusive Classroom Practice

Reviewing learning from a gender perspective

Reviewing learning from a disability perspective

Checklist for evaluating inclusion

School self-review and inclusion

Pupil review of inclusion

Inclusion review for headteachers

Inclusion review for INCO/SENCO

Inclusion review checklist for teachers (including NQTs)

Inclusion review for teaching assistants

Inclusion review for SEN/Inclusion governors

Inclusion review for parents/carers

Acknowledgements

The idea for producing *How to Create the Inclusive Classroom* arose from the many presentations I have made in LEAs and at national conferences in recent years. Educational professionals working in inclusive settings are constantly seeking practical resources, which will act as a good starting point in enabling them to remove barriers to learning and participation for a diversity of pupils.

This book should fill the gap that is currently apparent in terms of such practical resources. It clarifies expectations about applying inclusive learning principles and approaches, and supports the government's SEN Strategy and Inclusion Development Programme.

Inclusion can and does happen in a positive climate, where learners are empowered and given the opportunities to demonstrate their various strengths – this resource is a tool for shaping such an environment.

I wish to thank all the staff at David Fulton Publishers, and in particular Linda Evans, for continuing to give me the opportunity to share my inclusion knowledge and practical experiences with a wide audience.

Introduction

The government's SEN strategy emphasises:

"Inclusion is about the quality of children's experience; how they are helped to learn, achieve and participate fully in the life of the school."

(DfES 2004: page 25)

and acknowledges that:

"Difficulties in learning often arise from an unsuitable environment – inappropriate grouping of pupils, inflexible teaching styles, or inaccessible curriculum materials."

(DfES 2004: 2.1)

Personalised learning as an approach for pupils with SEN and disability may initially appear to be at odds with including the full diversity of learners in a class of thirty children. But, as schools become more inclusive, mainstream teachers will need to be able to respond to this wider range of needs in the classroom.

Introduction cont.

OfSTED and the DfES emphasise that effective teaching for children with SEN shares most of the characteristics of effective teaching for ALL children.

Effective inclusion does not entirely rely on specialist skills and resources. It requires:

- strong leadership from the headteacher in promoting inclusion;
- positive attitudes towards children who face difficulties in school;
- a greater responsiveness to meeting individual needs;
- a willingness among all staff to play an active part in inclusion;
- the creation of a positive learning environment.

Never underestimating the potential of any child is the starting point. Every child is good at something.

The aim of this book

The aim of this book is to enable all those involved in removing barriers to learning and achievement to know:

- what their roles and expectations are;
- how children and young people learn best;
- what good inclusive practice looks like in the classroom;
- how to empower inclusive learners;
- how to create an appropriate learning environment;
- how to promote learning skills across the curriculum.

Who the book is for

- Headteachers, and members of the school leadership team
- Inclusion Coordinators, SENCOs, all teachers, teaching assistants and practitioners working in early years settings, mainstream and special schools, units, PRUs, at all phases of education
- Those working in educational settings from learning support, health and social services
- Those involved in inclusion training in higher education, LEAs and schools
- LEA advisers, inspectors and consultants
- Educational psychologists.

How the format is designed to be used

- It can act as a quick point of reference for all teachers, and teaching assistants supporting pupils with SEN and disability

- Pages can be photocopied for professional development purposes, within the purchasing institution

- There is an accompanying CD which allows readers to download and customise templates on their computers.

Chapter 1

National Inclusion Framework

What makes inclusion work?

According to OfSTED (2003), the following key factors help schools to become more inclusive:

- a climate of acceptance of all pupils;
- careful preparation of placements for SEN pupils;
- availability of sufficient suitable teaching and personal support;
- widespread awareness among staff of the particular needs of SEN pupils and an understanding of the practical ways of meeting these needs in the classroom;
- sensitive allocation to teaching groups and careful curriculum modification, timetables and social arrangements;
- availability of appropriate materials and teaching aids and adapted accommodation;

What makes inclusion work? cont.

- an active approach to personal and social development, as well as to learning;

- well defined and consistently applied approaches to managing difficult behaviour;

- assessment, recording and reporting procedures which can embrace and express adequately the progress of pupils with more complex SEN who make only small gains in learning and PSD;

- involving parents/carers as fully as possible in decision-making, keeping them well informed about their child's progress and giving them as much practical support as possible;

- developing and taking advantage of training opportunities, including links with special schools and other schools.

(OfSTED 2003: 92)

Removing barriers to achievement

The government's strategy for SEN focuses on personalised learning as being an effective approach towards removing barriers to achievement.

Personalised learning relates to making education more responsive to individual children.

"Personalised learning embraces every aspect of school life, including teaching and learning strategies, ICT, curriculum choice, organisation and timetabling, assessment arrangements and relationships with the local community."

(DfES 2004: 3.1)

Removing barriers to achievement cont.

The principles of learning and teaching underpinning personalised learning should:

- set high expectations and give every learner confidence that they can succeed;
- establish what learners already know and build on it;
- structure and pace the learning experience to make it challenging and enjoyable;
- inspire learning through passion for the subject;
- make individuals active partners in their learning (assessment for learning); and
- develop learning skills and personal qualities.

(DfES 2004: 3.2)

Every child matters

Every Child Matters (DfES) clearly states its intention to reduce educational failure and maximise the potential of all children.

The promotion of full-service extended schools which open beyond school hours and provide breakfast clubs, after-school clubs and child care, and have health and social care support services on site, are recognised as being a positive development towards inclusion and removing barriers to achievement.

Access to out-of-school activities are valued because:

- they demonstrate that children's learning is not confined to the classroom;
- involvement in such activities contributes to children's holistic development;
- they help to re-engage young people who have had problems at school.

Disability, access and inclusion

A physical or mental disability includes:

- sensory impairments, severe disfigurements, hidden disabilities, e.g. mental illness/mental health problems, learning difficulties, dyslexia, diabetes, epilepsy.

Where:

- the effect of the disability lasts at least a year, and
- affects the child's ability to carry out normal daily activities.

A positive approach to SEN and disability is one where difference is valued for the enrichment it brings to the learning experiences of other able-bodied peers.

Access and inclusion
SEN and Disability Act 2001

CODE OF PRACTICE (Schools)

All teachers and early years practitioners should:

- not treat disabled children and young people less favourably;

- make reasonable steps to ensure that disabled children and young people are not placed at a substantial disadvantage compared to able-bodied peers;

- contribute towards producing a school Accessibility Plan, which makes progress towards:

  - improving access to the physical environment;

  - increasing curriculum access and participation; and

  - improving access to written information using alternative formats.

National Curriculum inclusion principles

Every teacher should implement the NC inclusion principles

Responding to pupils' diverse learning needs

Setting suitable learning challenges

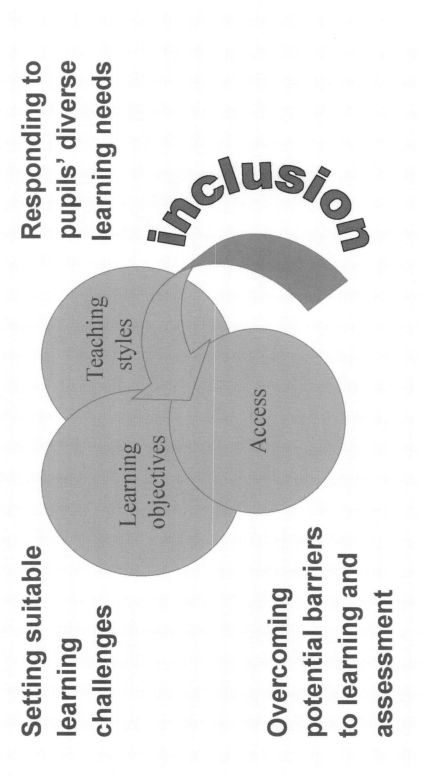

Overcoming potential barriers to learning and assessment

Assessment and Inclusion 1

- All children deserve to have their achievements and progression recognised and the curriculum should reflect the different levels of attainment likely to be achieved.

- Making use of the national P Scales for those pupils with complex SEN who are working towards National Curriculum Level 1, across the curriculum, ensures that the whole curriculum is accessed at an appropriate level.

- Teachers and TAs need to familiarise themselves with the P Scale assessment descriptors, and link these to their curriculum delivery, planning and IEP target setting.

- P Scales are an inclusive assessment tool which require exemplification and moderation, in order to validate judgements.

- P Scales also support the inclusion of dual-registered pupils who are educated across mainstream and special school settings.

- Using the national EBD scale provides a valuable assessment tool for recognising pupils' progress in learning, conduct and emotional behaviour.

Assessment and inclusion 2

The use of P scale level descriptors, like NC levels, helps to indicate expectation and progression in learning.

Data analysis of pupil performance helps to inform the allocation of additional SEN provision; it informs pupil groupings and highlights any anomalies or variations within a subject, or between different subjects.

Moderated P scale assessments aid the comparison of progress for pupils of similar ability at the same age with similar prior attainment, according to the relevant PLASC SEN category, across a range of educational settings. (Contextual issues such as teacher or pupil mobility need to be taken into account when making comparisons between schools.)

Moderation of P scales can also be supported effectively by video recording pupil achievements, and by maintaining portfolios of everyday learning experiences and outcomes for pupils with SEN.

Assessment, target setting and inclusion

"Setting challenging targets for pupils with SEN can help both pupils and schools focus their efforts and learning on achieving realistic goals."

(David Bell, Chief HMI, 2004)

Pupils need to identify their achievements through the use of their own preferred learning styles.

Teachers can support pupils' review of learning by enabling them to answer the following questions:

1) How well am I doing?
2) How well should I be doing?
3) What more should I aim to do?
4) What must I do to make progress, and meet targets set?
5) How do I know if the additional provision has been effective?

(OfSTED 2004: 18)

Features of the ideal inclusive school

Children and young people have identified that the ideal inclusive school should:

- value all pupils and acknowledge different personalities and gifts;

- have no league tables, and not compete with others;

- be safe, with swipe cards for the school gate;

- have anti-bullying alarms, first-aid classes and a key person to talk to about problems;

- be respectful, treat pupils as individuals, enable children and adults to talk freely to each other and value pupils' opinions;

- be flexible, without rigid timetables or exams or compulsory homework, and have no 'one-size-fits-all' curriculum.

(CSIE 2002)

Features of inclusive schools

OfSTED identified the following features of inclusive schools.

- Teaching, learning, achievement, attitudes and well-being of every young person matter
- Willing to offer new opportunities to pupils who have experienced previous failure
- Equality of opportunity, irrespective of age, gender, ethnicity, attainment and background
- Attention given to provision to meet full pupil diversity
- Inclusive in its policies, outlook and practices
- Zero tolerance of underachievement
- All teachers implement the NC inclusion principles.

(OfSTED 2000: 7)

SEN in mainstream inclusion checklist

- Effect and impact of teaching on SEN pupils' learning is good
- Work is matched to pupils' needs
- Effective use of ICT and multi-media is made
- Rate of progress made by pupils in view of their SEN is appropriate
- Practical IEPs are implemented, which promote learning
- Rationale for pupils' in-class support or withdrawal is clear
- Effective use of TAs improves pupils' learning
- Statement provision is being met
- Moderated assessment of pupils with SEN informs teacher planning
- Pupils are involved in target setting and review of progress
- Accessibility for pupils with SEN and disabilities promotes inclusion opportunities
- Impact of special school and support services interventions is good.

(OfSTED 2003: 96-97)

Chapter 2

Inclusive Classroom Practice

Inclusive learners' entitlement

Children and young people are entitled to:

- have ownership of their learning
- understand the learning process
- experience a range of multi-sensory learning styles
- develop their own tools for learning
- express their feelings, value judgements and emotional needs (developing emotional literacy).

Inclusive classroom climate

Early years practitioners, teachers, TAs and pupils need to develop their emotional literacy by:

- recognising the link between thoughts, feelings and reactions
- being able to manage emotions, i.e. what triggers them, how to handle them, monitoring self-talk
- recognising own strengths and weaknesses
- taking responsibility for decisions and actions
- learning to listen and ask questions appropriately
- learning skills such as co-operation, conflict resolution
- understanding negotiation and compromise
- learning the difference between assertiveness and aggression
- judging the consequences of alternative choices.

Including and empowering the pupils

Children's views deserve to be taken into account because they know better than anyone else which teaching and learning styles are successful, and which techniques of learning bring the best out of them. It is important that children and young people put their learning into practice.

Children and young people have a right to be heard and play a part in the decisions that affect them, according to the principles of the UN Convention on the Rights of the Child. Pupil participation is open to all, no matter what their race, religion, gender or disability.

Teachers don't have to be SEN specialists or super teachers. If they are prepared to listen to, and learn from, the pupils they teach, then children and young people will feel empowered, and barriers to achievement will be removed.

Empowering the SEN pupil

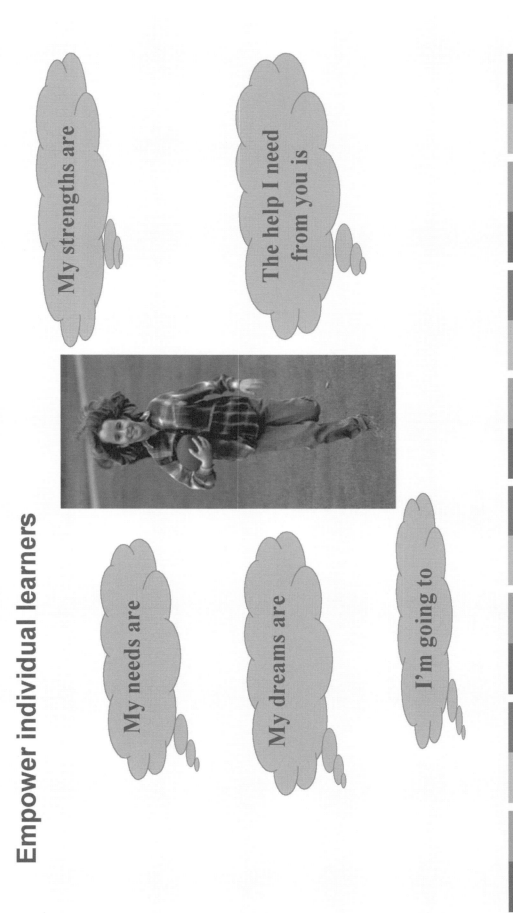

Empower individual learners

My strengths are

The help I need from you is

My needs are

My dreams are

I'm going to

Pupils' inclusive learning audit

As an inclusive learner:

- How do you prefer to learn?
- Where do you learn best?
- What helps you to learn?
- Who tells you most about how to learn?
- How could you improve your learning?
- When do you find learning difficult?
- What stops you learning in class?

Teachers' inclusive learning audit

- Do I have sufficient knowledge of pupils' learning styles?
- Which aspects of the subject are being learned well?
- Which aspects of the subject are not being understood and why?
- What does good teaching and learning look like in this subject?
- How do I teach pupils how to learn?
- How do I know pupils have learnt what I have taught them?
- How will I assess whether my chosen teaching strategies have been the most successful to use?
- What other strategies would have worked?

Inclusive learning – teacher checklist

How are you:

- ensuring that all pupils learn effectively?
- helping pupils to discuss the process of their learning?
- modelling good learning strategies?
- involving pupils in peer or self-assessment of their learning?
- using classroom displays interactively to enhance pupils' learning?
- involving TAs/LSAs in extending pupils' learning in-class?

Learning retention

On average, pupils remember:
20% of what is read
30% of what is heard
40% of what is seen displayed
50% of what is said or explained to others
60% of what is done in practical work
90% when all the above methods are used (multi-sensory learning)

Within 24 hours, without a review of learning
80% of new knowledge is lost.

Pupils' maximum concentration span is 2 minutes in excess of their chronological age, in minutes.

Effective inclusive learning approaches

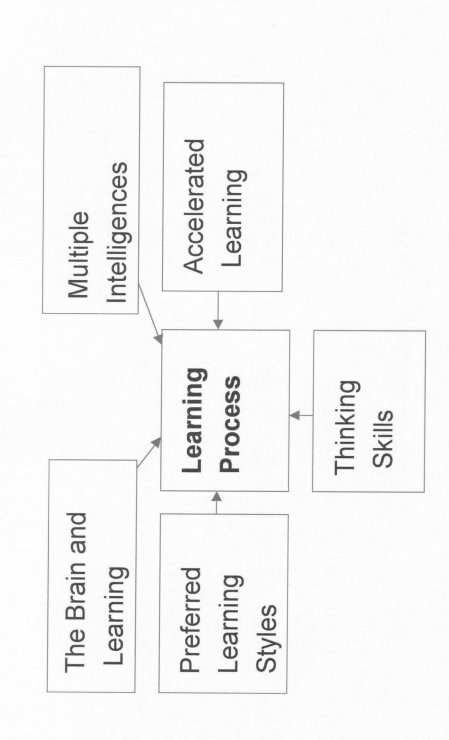

Learning styles

Include this in the pupil's learning log/IEP strategies

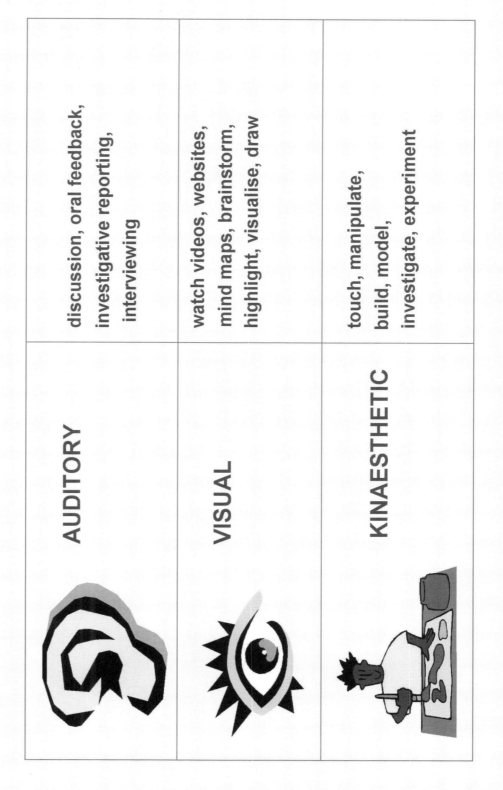

AUDITORY	discussion, oral feedback, investigative reporting, interviewing
VISUAL	watch videos, websites, mind maps, brainstorm, highlight, visualise, draw
KINAESTHETIC	touch, manipulate, build, model, investigate, experiment

The learning cycle

Include this in the pupil's learning log

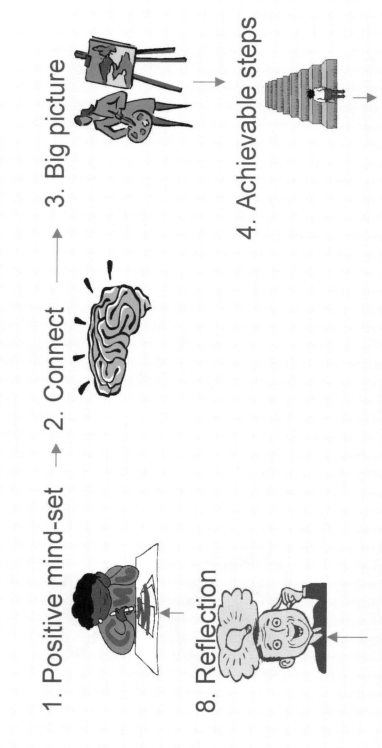

1. Positive mind-set → 2. Connect → 3. Big picture

4. Achievable steps

5. Input → 6. Main activity (explore) → Show knowledge

7. Show knowledge

8. Reflection

The learning cycle cont.

Positive mind-set: readiness for learning, emotionally secure climate

Connect the learning to previous learning and prior knowledge

Big picture: giving an overview of what is going to be learnt, and giving an outline of the learning objectives/expected outcomes

Achievable steps: breaking down learning into smaller stages

Input: using a range of multi-sensory learning approaches (VAK) – visual, auditory and kinaesthetic learning

Main activity: providing opportunities for using cross-curricular learning skills, e.g. experimenting; investigating; applying and using thinking skills and multiple intelligences; problem solving approaches; utilising whole-brain learning (pupils as active learners)

Show knowledge and understanding: explaining a concept, or three things learnt in the lesson, to another peer or to the teacher

Reflection: reviewing learning for recall and retention.

Accelerated learning approaches

Effective teaching strategies for the inclusive classroom, which help pupils to learn how to learn:

- Mind mapping – powerful tool for giving the 'big picture', connecting thinking and supporting memory recall

- Visualisation – guided visualisations stimulate imagination, support creative writing, mental rehearsal, relaxation, thought control and mood management

- Music – reduces stress, boosts memory, improves whole-brain thinking and increases learning capacity

- Multiple intelligences – promote understanding and mastery of learning

- Thinking skills – open-minded, problem solving, investigating and exploring alternative possibilities, questioning, evaluating, evidence gathering

- Brain gym, brain breaks – help refocus attention, reinforce concepts in learning, promote receptiveness to whole-brain learning, develop hand–eye coordination.

Whole-brain learning

LEFT BRAIN

(FEMALE)

Analytic

(language, logic, number, sequence)

Structured tasks

Clear instructions

Written information

RIGHT BRAIN

(MALE)

Intuitive, non-verbal

(visualisation, rhyme and rhythm, imagination)

Open-ended tasks

Self-selected tasks

Following hunches, guesses, intuition, impulses

Engage both sides of the brain at the same time.

Left- and right-brain activities

- Describe (left) a picture or diagram (right)

- Visualise (right) a written description (left)

- Convert text (left) into a picture (right)

- Turn key words (left) into a poem (right)

- Identify key words (left) and write them in a different colour (right).

Multiple intelligences for all learners

Attach this to pupil's IEP/ILP and highlight key strategies used

LINGUISTIC	brainstorming, discussing writing, word games
LOGICAL/MATHEMATICAL	problem solving, predict, classify, sequence, deduct
VISUAL SPATIAL	pictures, drawing diagrams video, displays, mind maps
KINAESTHETIC/BODILY	role play, movement, doing, modelling, games, brain gym
MUSICAL	singing, work to music, raps for memory
INTERPERSONAL	peer tutoring, team work role play, group projects
INTRAPERSONAL	reflection, solo study, targets, self-evaluation
NATURALISTIC	nature study, wildlife, ECO

Thinking skills for all pupils

Attach this to pupils IEPs/ILP and highlight strategies used

SYNTHESIS	create, compose, invent, design, forecast, be original, hypothesise
EVALUATION	judge, evaluate, give viewpoint, choose, prioritise
ANALYSIS	investigate, classify, compare and contrast fact/opinion
APPLICATION	demonstrate, use guides, maps, charts; construct
COMPREHENSION	restate, exemplify, explain, summarise, translate, edit, show
KNOWLEDGE	tell, recite, list, locate, define, remember

What inclusive classroom practice looks like

Children learn best when they:

- develop positive, secure, trusting relationships with their teacher, LSA/TA, learning mentor

- are learning predominantly in their preferred style

- use both sides of their brain

- know and understand the lesson objectives and expected learning outcomes

- have opportunities to ask and answer questions

- are actively involved in the learning process

- utilise ICT and multi-media technology across the curriculum, to demonstrate their knowledge, skills and understanding

- develop their thinking skills, utilise accelerated learning techniques

- utilise their cross-curricular study skills, e.g. mind mapping,

- have opportunities to regularly review their learning.

Ideas for promoting inclusive practice

- Introduce learning logs for pupils

- Set a puzzle, problem or word of the week to resolve or define

- Design IEPs on CD, reduce paperwork and promote E-learning

- Embed buddy systems, mentoring, circle time, circle of friends

- Re-name classrooms – OASIS (Open Access Supporting Inclusive Study), or the Learning Zone

- Produce inclusion guidance packs and information in multi-media formats for staff, written from the perspective of a pupil with SEN

- Produce training CD or video for staff, pupils, parents on aspects of SEN, disability and inclusion, e.g. a day in the life of a pupil with ASD in school

- Run an inclusion activities day(s), week, Easter, Summer or Saturday school, in partnership with a special school

- Hold joint special/mainstream school induction, transition and taster days for dual placement pupils and their parents.

Reducing barriers to learning and participation

1. Identify the pupil's current level of attainment

2. Identify their preferred learning style(s) and strengths

3. Focus on what their priority targets are in relation to: communication and interaction; cognition and learning; behaviour, emotional and social development; sensory and/or physical development

4. Ensure teaching approaches match pupils' preferred learning style(s) and that they inform the IEP strategies which enable the pupil with SEN to access the curriculum and meet their set targets

5. Use the learning cycle in lessons

6. Provide an appropriate, emotionally secure learning environment.

Inclusive individual education plans

In order to make IEPs more positive, meaningful and inclusive they should indicate on them:

- the pupil's preferred learning style(s)
- how the pupil's preferred learning style(s) informs the access strategies to enable targets to be met
- the pupil's strengths and talents
- the pupil's level of attainment (learning/behaviour) P scales, PIVATS, NC level

How accessible is your classroom? 1

- Can all pupils see the board, TV monitor, teacher modelling or pupil role-play activities?

- Can bright light be dimmed or cut out by window blinds?

- Can pupils, especially those in wheelchairs, move around the classroom safely?

- Are resources clearly labelled?

- Is the classroom atmosphere calm?

- Is classroom furniture and equipment the right height for disabled pupils?

- Is there a quiet, distraction-free area in the classroom for some pupils?

How accessible is your classroom? 2

- Is use made of visual timetables?

- Is written information produced in a range of multi-media formats?

- Is extra time given to those who need it, to complete tasks set?

- Are you fully aware of how a pupil's disability may impact on their learning and behaviour?

- Are any pupil misunderstandings, misconceptions and mistakes dealt with sensitively and positively?

The Government's Strategy for SEN

The Inclusion Development Programme will focus on removing barriers to achievement for those children who place the greatest demands on mainstream schools, in relation to inclusion.

These children include those with:

Autistic Spectrum Disorder (ASD)

Behavioural, Emotional and Social Difficulties (BESD)

Speech, Language and Communication Difficulties (SLCD)

Moderate Learning Difficulties (MLD)

Each type of SEN presents particular challenges for mainstream teachers. The following practical classroom strategies will enable staff to ensure curriculum accessibility.

Classroom strategies for including pupils with ASD

- Give one instruction at a time, and ask ASD pupil to repeat back
- Use symbols, pictorial instructions, visual timetables
- Introduce one task at a time and provide clear targets
- Give the pupil extra time to process information and complete tasks
- Make good use of ICT and musical rhymes/songs to reinforce instructions and learning
- Prepare pupils in advance for any change in classroom routines
- In teaching activities make use of pupils' interests, strengths, and skills
- Provide a calm, quiet, distraction-free work area in the classroom
- Use simple consistent language, some closed questions and repetition
- Encourage turn-taking activities, utilise circle time and social stories
- Give the ASD pupil a responsible role and provide peer partners
- Provide the ASD pupil with a key adult 'listener' (staff member).

(©Association of Teachers and Lecturers 2002: 46-47)

Classroom strategies for including pupils with BESD 1

- Catch the pupil being good and emphasise the positives
- Give the pupil a classroom responsibility to raise self-esteem
- Refer pupils regularly to classroom code of conduct, whole class targets, and use consistently
- Play calming music to increase work output, where appropriate
- Give breaks between tasks, e.g. do brain gym
- Provide opportunities for practical activities/experiential learning, use of ICT, multi-media
- Make expectations explicit for behaviour and learning by setting clear targets, and by giving clear explanations
- Make use of different seating and grouping arrangements for different activities
- Allow the pupil 'time-out' or a cooling-off period
- Create a positive learning environment that adopts a 'no-blame' approach, based on mutual respect and high expectations.

53

Classroom strategies for including pupils with BESD 2

- Personalise teaching, relating work to pupils' interests
- Communicate in a calm, clear manner, making eye-contact and avoiding confrontation
- Use deliberate silence, only starting lessons when every pupil is paying attention
- Make use of visible, pupil-friendly behaviour and anger-management systems, e.g. traffic lights, behaviour gauge
- Listen to the pupil, always giving them a chance to explain the reason for their misbehaviour
- Use humour sensitively to deflect any confrontation
- Keep instructions, routines and rules short, precise and positive
- Make use of how, why, what if questions to keep pupils on task
- Allow pupils to make responsible behaviour choices for themselves.

(© Association of Teachers and Lecturers 2002: 51–52)

Classroom strategies for including pupils with SLCD 1

- Keep information short, simple, straightforward
- Avoid speaking quickly and speak clearly
- Pair the pupil up with a good peer language role model, and with a supportive group of friends
- Work on improving concentration by building up step-by-step the pupils' listening time, i.e. listening to radio programmes
- Give the pupil simple messages to take (verbal and written)
- Use open questioning
- Read aloud and use commentary to improve pupils' listening skills
- Use discussion and visual cues to support written communication.

Classroom strategies for including pupils with SLCD 2

- Use props to encourage pupils to talk more, e.g. telephone, audio-tape recorder, video

- Provide key vocabulary/word lists

- Engage the pupil in sequencing and matching activities to develop language

- Teach language skills through games, e.g. 20 questions, role play conversations, guessing games using verbal cues

- Provide a quiet area in the classroom for talking and listening activities

- Use shorter sentences.

(©Association of Teachers and Lecturers 2002: 43–44)

Classroom strategies for including pupils with learning difficulties (MLD, Sp.LD) 1

- Allow the pupil to work at their own pace in order to process learning
- Structure learning in smaller steps, break down tasks into smaller components
- Present the same concept in different ways to reinforce learning
- Provide opportunities for routine learning, repetition
- Model, demonstrate what you want the pupil to do
- Provide breaks between tasks, and work towards increasing concentration
- Support writing with mind maps, writing frames, prompt cards, word lists, pictures
- Check pupils' understanding by asking them to repeat what they have been asked to do, or state three things they have learnt in the lesson.

Classroom strategies for including pupils with learning difficulties (MLD, Sp.LD) 2

- Allow the pupil to present their work outcomes in a variety of different ways, e.g. multi-media, ICT
- Give the pupil opportunities to display their talents and experience success
- Provide immediate positive praise to reward effort and achievement
- Use real experiences, objects and artefacts to consolidate learning
- Give the pupil step-by-step instructions and not too many at once
- Utilise VAK (multi-sensory) learning approaches, vary activities
- Provide opportunities for pair, group, whole class and independent learning.

(©Association of Teachers and Lecturers 2002: 10–12)

Chapter 3

Inclusion Roles and Expectations

In line with the SEN Code of Practice which commented that:

"All teachers are teachers of pupils with special educational needs",

the government's strategy for SEN states:

"All teachers should expect to teach children with SEN."

The government wants to see:

- all teachers having the skills and confidence – and access to specialist advice where necessary – to help children with SEN to reach their potential;

- practical teaching and learning resources to help teachers expand their repertoire of inclusive teaching skills and strategies and plan confidently to include children with increasingly complex needs;

- help for SENCOs, literacy and numeracy coordinators to support children with dyslexia;

- guidance for key staff – e.g. SENCO training on managing and monitoring effective learning for SEN pupils in secondary schools.

Headteacher role and expectations

The government's strategy for SEN states:

" … headteachers should ensure that staff develop the skills and confidence to respond effectively to children's SEN."

(DfES 2004: 2.8)

The headteacher is responsible for:

- the daily management of all aspects of the school's work, including provision for SEN children;
- working closely with the school's SENCO/INCO;
- keeping the governing body fully informed about SEN/inclusion;
- leading and developing a vision for inclusion within the school;
- ensuring that the school improvement plan and subject plans include a SEN and inclusion priority;
- ensuring SEN and inclusion features on key meeting agendas;
- checking the quality of teaching and learning.

SENCO role and expectations

The government's strategy for SEN states:

"SENCOs play a pivotal role, co-ordinating provision across the school and linking class and subject teachers with SEN specialists to improve the quality of teaching and learning."

(DfES 2004: 3.14)

SENCOs need to be visible, with high expectations; able to empower other staff, and to provide the impetus for change.

SENCOs need to check if their job description mentions inclusion, and clarify what the headteacher's expectation of the SENCO role is, in the context of inclusion within the school.

SENCO role and inclusion

The Index for Inclusion raises the following issues for SENCOs:

- Role clarification: SENCO, Learning Support Coordinator or Inclusion Coordinator (INCO)?

- SEN Policy or Inclusion Policy?

- SEN replaced by the term *"barriers to learning and participation"* or Additional Educational Needs (AEN)?

- SENCO member of the school's Inclusion Coordinating Group?

SENCO's evolving inclusion role

- From individual SEN pupil focus to focus on classroom practice for a diversity of learners

- From diagnostic assessment to collaborative problem-solving and assessment for learning

- From placement on isolated specific programmes to inclusive teaching and learning approaches and strategies

- From working in isolation to partnership and teamwork

- From conventional traditional role to 'risk taking', 'thinking outside the box', innovation, creativity and seeking new opportunities.

SENCO/INCO role

- Advise on curriculum differentiation and accessibility issues
- Support teacher planning to meet pupil diversity
- Advise on inclusive teaching and learning approaches
- Model good SEN and inclusive classroom practice
- Monitor the quality and effectiveness of SEN/Inclusion policy and provision
- Support the implementation of the NC inclusion statement of principles
- Advise on the efficient and effective deployment of TAs, SEN staff
- Help other colleagues to sustain constructive working relationships between pupils and staff
- Contribute to SEN/Inclusion INSET and monitor its impact on pupils' learning
- Maintain productive partnerships with parents of SEN pupils
- Collaborate with other subject coordinators and develop their skills.

NQTs' roles and expectations

The government's strategy for SEN states in relation to NQTs and QTS that they must demonstrate that they can:

- Understand their responsibilities under the SEN Code of Practice, and know how to seek advice from specialists on less common types of SEN;

- Differentiate their teaching to meet the needs of pupils, including those with SEN;

- Identify and support pupils who experience BESD;

- Not discriminate against disabled pupils

- Spend time with the SENCO to focus on specific and general SEN matters

- Demonstrate that they plan effectively to meet the needs of their pupils in their classes with SEN, with or without statements.

(DfES 2004: 3.11)

Teachers' roles and expectations 1

- Measure and monitor the ongoing progress in learning, behaviour and PSD for pupils with SEN

- Identify and reduce barriers to learning

- Differentiate the curriculum to provide maximum access

- Follow the guidance of national strategies

- Discuss planning with additional support staff

- Discuss progress of pupils with SEN with SENCO, TAs, Learning Mentors

- Utilise a range of teaching strategies to match pupils' preferred learning styles.

Teachers' roles and expectations 2

- Devise strategies with the SENCO to support pupils IEP implementation

- Ensure pupils know their IEP targets

- Link IEPs to teacher planning

- Understand the collaborative partnership of TA and teacher, in meeting the diverse needs of pupils in the inclusive classroom

- Know and implement the NC inclusion statement of principles consistently

- Understand and follow the graduated response for pupils with SEN

- Teach pupils how to learn

- Have high expectations of pupils with SEN

- Use appropriate assessment.

Teaching Assistants' roles and expectations

- Know all about the special needs of pupils they support
- Enhance access to the mainstream lesson
- Reinforce and extend pupils' learning by using VAK approaches
- Make use of open questioning and encourage pupils to talk about their knowledge and understanding
- Provide opportunities for pupils to share ideas and demonstrate their knowledge and understanding
- Keep pupils on task
- Provide a balance between intervention and encouragement of pupil independence
- Briefly record the nature and impact of support provided to pupils
- Know what the objectives for the lesson are and the teacher's expected learning outcomes for pupils with SEN
- Plan with teachers for effective differentiation of the curriculum
- Discuss jointly pupil progress and achievements.

Effective deployment of TAs

Teachers should:

- Meet regularly with the TA to discuss planning and pupils' targets
- Make good use of the TA's knowledge of pupils with SEN
- Value the TA's contribution by utilising their talents and strengths
- Discuss pupil progress with the TA
- Give positive feedback to TA in relation to their support role
- Work with TA to ensure their SEN support interventions utilise mind-friendly approaches (VAK).

The government's strategy for SEN comments:

"It is important that teachers and LSAs play complementary roles.

(DfES 2004: 3.16)

Pupils' roles and expectations

The government's strategy for SEN comments:

"Involving SEN children in decisions about their own learning, IEP reviews, transition arrangements and in ways of removing barriers to their learning, will help to develop their life skills such as problem-solving and negotiation."

(DfES 2004: 3.38–3.39)

The pupil's role is to:

- Act as a peer buddy, mentor or mediator to pupils with SEN
- Provide a positive role model for younger pupils in school
- Accept and tolerate difference and diversity in other pupils
- Understand and be sensitive towards the feelings of others
- Work cooperatively with other pupils
- Show respect for adults and other pupils
- Make responsible choices in relation to behaviour and learning
- Avoid 'put downs' towards other pupils who experience learning difficulties.

Parents'/carers' roles and expectations 1

Charles Clarke, Secretary of State for Education and Skills comments:

"Parents must be able to have confidence that their children's needs will be met quickly and effectively throughout their education . . . "

(DfES 2004: foreword)

Parents need to be reassured that:

- teachers will value the contribution of parents/carers in relation to the knowledge they have about their own child;

- teachers will respect and listen to the views of parents/carers;

- the school will give the parents/carers the opportunity to consult with relevant staff;

- information about the school and their child's progress will be given in parent-friendly language and different formats to suit parents' preferred means of communication;

- Teachers/TAs understand their child's SEN and/or medical needs;

- They will be directed to other sources of support and advice;

- Their enquiries will be dealt with quickly.

Parents'/carers' roles and expectations 2

OfSTED comments that parents of SEN pupils expect schools to show a: *"Commitment to success, optimism, clarity of expectations, availability of support and sheer persistence."*

(OfSTED 2003: 71)

Parents' responsibilities are to:

- take an interest in their child's education;
- listen to their child's worries and anxieties;
- support homework and out-of-hours learning activities;
- ensure their child attends school regularly;
- inform their child's teacher if their child is worried about aspects of school life or work;
- request work from the school in instances where their child is likely to be absent for some time from school.

Governing body role and expectations 1

"Inclusion ... requires ownership by the head teacher and senior management team, governors and all staff."

(DfES 2004: 4.9)

The SEN Code of Practice is explicit about the governors' role:

- ensure that the necessary provision is made for SEN pupils
- ensure the pupils' SEN are made known to those teaching them
- ensure teachers in the school know the importance of identifying and providing for pupils with SEN
- ensure SEN pupils join in the activities of the school together with pupils who do not have SEN, as far as is reasonably practical
- report to parents on the implementation of the school's SEN policy
- ensure parents are informed that their child is receiving SEN provision.

(DfES 2001: 1:21–1:22)

Governing body role and expectations 2

- Involved fully in developing and monitoring the quality and effectiveness of the school's SEN policy and provision

- Are knowledgeable and up-to-date about the school's strengths and areas for further development in relation to SEN provision

- Know how funding, equipment and personnel resources are deployed, and their impact on raising standards (value added)

- Meet regularly with the SENCO/INCO to receive regular up-dates on progress in SEN/inclusion

- Are aware of the priorities and the school's Accessibility Plan, and the progress made towards meeting these

- Check the impact of SEN/Inclusion INSET on improving classroom practice

- Check that the school is supporting parents/carers of SEN pupils

- Check that SEN and inclusion is an integral part of the SIP.

Outreach/external professionals' roles and expectations 1

The government's strategy for SEN wants to see SEN advisory and support services, including outreach, provided by special and mainstream schools as:

"extending SEN advice and support to early years settings, including those in the private and voluntary sectors;

increasingly offering advice and support on a preventative basis, so reducing the need for statements;

supporting the development of inclusive practice in all schools and early years settings;

making the best use of existing specialist provision including special schools and specialist resource bases and units in mainstream schools."

(DfES 2004:2.37)

Outreach/external professionals' roles and expectations 2

- Provide schools and early years settings with advice, guidance and consultancy
- Model, demonstrate and disseminate good inclusive practice
- Coach and mentor exemplary staff to become 'Leading Inclusion Teachers/TAs' to work across schools
- Support inclusion initiatives within schools/clusters
- Support the inclusion capacity building of mainstream schools
- Promote inclusion partnerships between special and mainstream schools
- Provide 'bespoke' school and LEA Inclusion training
- Advise schools on inclusion self-review and policy
- Produce inclusion handbooks and guidance materials
- Support the development of multi-professional working, e.g. full-service extended schools.

Transition, SEN and inclusion

The promotion of smooth transition from KS2 to KS3 can be improved by:

- holding presentation evenings for Year 6 parents which focus on what to expect at the secondary school, e.g. video presentations on 'a day in the life of a Year 7 pupil at High School', with pupil commentary and visual images of school life depicted from the pupil's perspective;

- delivering lively visual presentations to Year 6 and Year 5 pupils on what to expect on moving to secondary school;

- holding after-school transition sessions for any anxious Year 6 pupils, which will provide a smaller forum for demystifying the secondary school;

- summer term presentation from Year 7 pupils to Year 6 pupils on what it was like starting secondary school;

- transfer of pupils' portfolios of work and achievements

- holding a transition team-building day outside school for Year 7 pupils, in order to support the development of collaborative team work/friendships.

Chapter 4

Reviewing Inclusive Classroom Practice

QCA provided a useful guide for reviewing the learning of different groups of pupils within the context of the inclusive classroom.

When reviewing learning for those pupils with SLCD ensure that:

- alternative methods of communication have enabled them to demonstrate their learning, e.g. use of signing, symbols (PECS), ICT/multi-media;

- accessible curriculum materials have been made available for these pupils at all levels of attainment, to ensure learning takes place;

- assessment arrangements have ensured SLCD pupils have been able to demonstrate their understanding and attainments;

- the different paths that learning may take for some of these learners have been clearly identified.

Reviewing learning from a gender perspective

- Work set has catered for the different learning styles of girls and boys
- Curriculum materials and teaching procedures are free from gender discrimination and stereotyping
- There is a balance between practical and theoretical learning approaches
- Teaching and learning approaches interest, motivate and engage girls and boys of different ages, and from different backgrounds and ability ranges
- The demands placed on language skills (reading and writing), in a range of subjects, do not disadvantage or de-motivate boys, in particular
- There is a balance between open-ended, process-based assessment and assessment based on memorising facts or rules
- Girls and boys have opportunities to develop their understanding and skills of formal assessment techniques (self-assessment).

Reviewing learning from a disability perspective

- Learning materials and resources have been modified for those who are physically disabled or sensory impaired

- There are tactile materials, Braille text, taped materials available for the assessment of pupils with VI

- Curriculum materials have been developed for HI pupils at all levels of attainment that match their language development

- Special assessment papers for HI pupils are available

- Disabled pupils are able to use technological aids, and alternative methods of communication in their assessment and learning

- The greater length of time needed and the extra physical effort and concentration required by learners with physical, medical and sensory impairments have been taken into account and valued.

Checklist for evaluating inclusion

- All pupils are getting a fair deal in the school, and in all lessons
- All teachers are identifying and overcoming barriers to learning, achievement and participation
- The school's ethos and practice does promote inclusion
- The school's inclusion strengths and areas for further development are clear
- Inclusion is having a positive impact on pupils' learning
- All teachers are implementing the NC inclusion principles consistently
- All teachers are addressing any pupil under-achievement
- The school and the staff know what they must do in order to improve their inclusive practice
- The school and the staff have got the capacity to improve their inclusive culture, policy and practice.

School self-review and inclusion

- Pupil performance data is being analysed and used to address any pupil under-achievement.

- Grouping, setting and withdrawal arrangements are inclusive.

- The SMT/subject leaders monitor and track pupil progress.

- Work in lessons is challenging pupils sufficiently.

- Staff INSET has impacted on improving inclusive practice

- Discrimination, any negative attitudes and stereotyping are being challenged and overcome.

- Foundation Stage Curriculum, National Curriculum and out-of-hours learning activities do embrace cultural diversity and equal opportunities.

Pupil review of inclusion

1. I like being at this school
2. I find out new things in lessons
3. Lessons are interesting and fun
4. I get help when I get stuck with my work
5. I have to work hard
6. Teachers do show me how to make my work better
7. Other children in my class behave well
8. Other children in the class are friendly towards me
9. There is an adult I can go to if I am worried at school
10. Teachers do treat me fairly
11. Teachers do listen to my ideas
12. I am trusted to do things on my own at school and in lessons.

Inclusion review for headteachers

- Inclusion is viewed positively by all pupils and staff in school
- Inclusion offers new and exciting challenges and opportunities
- The school's inclusion policy is clear and guides practice
- Whole-school coordination, monitoring and evaluation of inclusion is effective
- The INCO/SENCO is well-supported by the headteacher
- The SIP features an inclusion/SEN priority, which is reflected in all subject development plans
- Implementation of the school's Accessibility Plan is progressing
- All pupils have an opportunity to review their own progress and have a say in their learning provision
- Parents'/carers' views are noted and acted upon
- The SEN/Inclusion Governor is proactive and monitors the quality and impact of inclusion provision with the INCO/SENCO
- All pupils make good progress and reach their optimum potential, in relation to prior attainment, and their SEN.

Inclusion review for INCO/SENCO 1

- Sufficient non-contact time is provided to coordinate, monitor and evaluate inclusion/SEN provision throughout the school

- The INCO/SENCO is well-supported in their role by the SMT

- The INCO/SENCO meets regularly with KS and subject coordinators, Year Heads and Inclusion/SEN representatives to discuss pupil progress, and target further intervention

- The INCO/SENCO meets regularly with the Inclusion/SEN governor to report on progress

- The INCO/SENCO leads a team of TAs/LSAs effectively, and meets with them regularly to monitor impact of interventions, and identify inclusion CPD needs for staff

- The analysis of pupil performance data and evidence from reviews informs curriculum access and provision required.

Inclusion review for INCO/SENCO 2

- Parents/carers are kept informed by regular communication, in preferred form, about their child's progress and provision

- Pupils are involved in target setting, reviewing their own progress and additional provision

- The additional resources for SEN and inclusion are reviewed in relation to their impact on raising standards

- Future inclusion and SEN priorities are identified by surveys and discussions with all stakeholders, e.g. parents, pupils, staff

- The INCO/SENCO has access to appropriate CPD to support their role.

Inclusion review checklist for teachers (including NQTs) 1

ALL TEACHERS:

- know and understand the barriers to learning encountered by pupils

- recognise pupils' preferred learning styles

- utilise a range of teaching approaches to remove barriers to achievement (VAK)

- ensure pupils have opportunities to work in pairs, groups, as a whole class, and individually

- are clear about the role and expectations of TAs, Learning Mentors, peer buddies, peer mediators in the classroom

- utilise positive praise with pupils, and enable them to make responsible choices in relation to behaviour and learning

- refer pupils to the classroom learning and behaviour code, and ensure this is used consistently and effectively.

Inclusion review checklist for teachers (including NQTs) 2

ALL TEACHERS:

- implement the NC inclusion statement of principles consistently in lessons

- create an appropriate emotionally literate classroom climate

- apply the knowledge and skills from inclusion training to their classroom practice, and ensure this impacts positively on pupils' learning

- receive good practical advice, support and guidance from the INCO/SENCO in school

- utilise and apply ICT, multi-media effectively during lessons, across the curriculum, in order to enhance pupils' learning access and outcomes.

Inclusion review for teaching assistants

- All staff, including TAs are clear about each other's role
- The impact and effectiveness of TA support and interventions are documented, monitored and evaluated.

TAs:

- are well supported in their role by the INCO/SENCO
- have quality time with teachers to feed back on support outcomes and pupil progress
- make significant contributions to the review of pupils' IEPs, IBPs, ILPs, and reviews of progress
- are clear about the school's current SEN and Inclusion priorities
- meet regularly as a team with the INCO/SENCO to discuss pupil progress and identify future TA CPD requirements
- are given the opportunity to utilise their talents and subject interests within their support role and in out-of-hours learning
- are valued and respected members of an inclusive learning team
- have the opportunity to share and observe good inclusive practice.

Inclusion review for SEN/Inclusion governors

- The nominated governor attends regular training on SEN and Inclusion, and keeps up to date with developments

- The role of the SEN/Inclusion governor is clear

- The SEN/Inclusion governor meets regularly with the SENCO/INCO to receive up-dates and reviews about inclusion and SEN developments within the school

- The SEN/Inclusion governor supports the SENCO/INCO in monitoring SEN/Inclusion policy and provision within the school

- The SEN/Inclusion governor knows the impact that additional SEN and inclusion resources have on pupils' learning

- The SEN/Inclusion governor is fully involved in the review and implementation of the school's Accessibility Plan

- The SEN/Inclusion governor acts as a 'critical friend' and their contributions are valued.

Inclusion review for parents/carers

- The school's inclusion priorities are known to parents/carers
- The school's strengths in inclusion are known and the school has a good reputation for inclusion in the local community
- Parents/carers have an opportunity to contribute to the school's inclusion activities and decision-making
- The school has productive inclusion partnerships with other schools, local businesses and the community
- The school has an inclusion policy in parent-friendly language
- The key member of staff responsible for inclusion is known to parents and acts as a first point of contact
- Parents/carers are made welcome when visiting the school
- Staff are polite when parents telephone the school
- The school's inclusion expectations are made clear
- The school works positively in partnership with parents/carers.

Abbreviations

AEN	Additional Educational Needs
ASD	Autistic Spectrum Disorder
ATL	Association of Teachers and Lecturers
BESD	Behavioural, Emotional and Social Difficulties
CPD	Continuing Professional Development
CSIE	Centre for Studies on Inclusive Education
DfES	Department for Education and Skills
EBD	Emotional and Behavioural Difficulties
HI	Hearing Impairment
IBP	Individual Behaviour Plan
IEP	Individual Education Plan
ILP	Inclusive Learning Plan
INCO	Inclusion Coordinator

Abbreviations cont.

INSET	In-service Education and Training
KS	Key Stage
LEA	Local Education Authority
LSA	Learning Support Assistant
MLD	Moderate Learning Difficulties
NC	National Curriculum
NQT	Newly Qualified Teacher
OASIS	Open Access Supporting Inclusive Study
OfSTED	Office for Standards in Education
PECS	Picture Exchange Communication System
PLASC	Pupil Level Annual School Census
PRU	Pupil Referral Unit
PSD	Personal and Social Development
QCA	Qualifications and Curriculum Authority

Abbreviations cont.

SEN — Special Educational Needs

SENCO — Special Educational Needs Coordinator

SIP — School Improvement Plan

SLCD — Speech, Language, and Communication Difficulties

SMT — Senior Management Team

Sp.LD — Specific Learning Difficulties

TA — Teaching Assistant

UN — United Nations

VAK — Visual, Auditory and Kinaesthetic

VI — Visual Impairment

Useful websites

http://inclusion.ngfl.gov.uk

http://www.inclusive-solutions.com

http://www.nc.uk.net

http://www.teachernet.gov.uk/sen

http://www.qca.org.uk/ages3-14/6166.html

http://www.educational-psychologist.co.uk/interventions.htm

http://www.nasen.org.uk

http://www.csie.org.uk

http://www.ace-ed.org.uk

http://www.parentsforinclusion.org

http://www.parents.dfes.gov.uk

References and further reading 1

ACCAC (2000) *A Structure for Success: Guidance on the National Curriculum and Autistic Spectrum Disorder.* Cardiff: The Qualifications, Curriculum and Assessment Authority for Wales.

ATL (2002) *Achievement for All: Working with Children with Special Educational Needs in Mainstream Schools and Colleges.* London: Association of Teachers and Lecturers.

Audit Commission (2002) *Special Educational Needs: A Mainstream Issue.* London: Audit Commission.

Booth, T. and Ainscow, M. (2002) *Index for Inclusion: Developing Learning and Participation in Schools.* Bristol: Centre for Studies on Inclusive Education.

Daines, B., Fleming, P. and Miller, C. (1996) *Spotlight on Special Educational Needs: Speech and Language Difficulties.* Tamworth: National Association for Special Educational Needs.

DfEE (1999) *From Exclusion to Inclusion: A Report of the Disability Rights Task Force on Civil Rights for Disabled People.* London: Department for Education and Employment.

References and further reading 2

DfEE (1999) *The National Curriculum: Handbook for Primary Teachers in England.* London: Department for Education and Employment.

DfES (2001) *Special Educational Needs Code of Practice.* London: Department for Education and Skills.

DfES (2002) *Including All Children in the Literacy Hour and Daily Mathematics Lesson: Management Guide.* London: Department for Education and Skills.

DfES (2003) *Every Child Matters – Summary.* London: Department for Education and Skills.

DfES (2003) *Working Together: Giving Children and Young People a Say.* London: Department for Education and Skills.

DfES (2004) *Removing Barriers to Achievement. The Government's Strategy for SEN.* London: Department for Education and Skills.

DEE (2002) *Inclusion in Schools Course Book.* London: Disability Equality in Education.

Disability Rights Commission (DRC) (2002) *Code of Practice for Schools.*

References and further reading 3

Disability Discrimination Act 1995: Part 4. London: The Stationery Office.

Dryden, G. and Vos, J. (2001) *The Learning Revolution: To Change the Way the World Learns.* Stafford: Network Educational Press.

Ealing Education Services (2002) *Inclusion: A Celebration of Good Practice in Ealing.* London: Ealing Education Department, Access and Inclusion, Inspection and Advisory Divisions.

Hughes, M. (1999) *Closing the Learning Gap.* Stafford: Network Educational Press.

NCB (2002) *Making It Work: Removing Disability Discrimination – Are You Ready?* Hertfordshire: National Children's Bureau.

OfSTED (2000) *Evaluating Educational Inclusion: Guidance for Inspectors and Schools.* London: Office for Standards in Education.

OfSTED (2003) *Inspecting Schools: Handbook for Inspecting Secondary Schools.* London: Office for Standards in Education.

OfSTED (2003) *Special Educational Needs in the Mainstream: LEA Policy and Support Services* (HMI 556) London: Office for Standards in Education.

References and further reading 4

OfSTED (2003) *Special Educational Needs in the Mainstream* (HMI 511) London: Office for Standards in Education.

OfSTED (2003) *Pupils with Emotional, Behavioural and Social Difficulties in Mainstream Schools. Special Educational Needs in the Mainstream: Annex 2.* London: Office for Standards in Education.

OfSTED (2003) *Pupils with Autistic Spectrum Disorder in Mainstream Schools. Special Educational Needs in the Mainstream: Annex 4.* London: Office for Standards in Education.

OfSTED (2004) *Setting Targets for Pupils with Special Educational Needs* (HMI 751) London: Office for Standards in Education.

QCA (2001) *Supporting School Improvement. Emotional and Behavioural Development.* London: Qualifications and Curriculum Authority.

QCA (2002) *Including All Learners.* London: Qualifications and Curriculum Authority.

Scoles, K. (2002) *'Can anyone tell me what was "special" about my special schools?'* Bristol: Centre for Studies on Inclusive Education.

Shaw, L. (2002) *We Want To Be Together.* Bristol: Centre for Studies on Inclusive Education.

References and further reading 5

Smith, A. and Call, N. (2000) *The ALPS Approach: Accelerated Learning in Primary Schools.* Stafford: Network Educational Press.

Shaw, S. and Hawes, T. (1998) *Effective Teaching and Learning in the Primary Classroom: A Practical Guide to Brain-compatible Learning.* Leicester: Optimal Learning.

Tod, J. and Blamires, M. (1998) *Individual Education Plans: Speech and Language.* London: David Fulton Publishers.

TTA (1999) *National Special Educational Needs Specialist Standards.* London: Teacher Training Agency.

TTA (2003) *Induction Standards – TTA Guidance for Newly Qualified Teachers.* London: Teacher Training Agency.

TTA (2003) *Into Induction.* London: Teacher Training Agency.